# SIMPLE OBJECT LESSONS
# FOR YOUNG CHILDREN

## Object Lessons Series

Bess, C. W., *Object-Centered Children's Sermons*, 0734-8
Bess, C. W., *Sparkling Object Sermons for Children*, 0824-7
Bess, C. W., & Roy DeBrand, *Bible-Centered Object Sermons for Children*, 0886-7
Biller, Tom & Martie, *Simple Object Lessons for Children*, 0793-3
Bruinsma, Sheryl, *Easy-to-Use Object Lessons*, 0832-8
Bruinsma, Sheryl, *New Object Lessons*, 0775-5
Bruinsma, Sheryl, *Object Lessons for Every Occasion*, 0994-4
Bruinsma, Sheryl, *Object Lessons for Special Days*, 0920-0
Bruinsma, Sheryl, *Object Lessons for Very Young Children*, 0956-1
Claassen, David, *Object Lessons for a Year*, 2514-1
Connelly, H. W., *47 Object Lessons for Youth Programs*, 2314-9
Coombs, Robert, *Concise Object Sermons for Children*, 2541-9
Coombs, Robert, *Enlightening Object Lessons for Children*, 2567-2
Cooper, Charlotte, *50 Object Stories for Children*, 2523-0
Cross, Luther, *Easy Object Stories*, 2502-8
Cross, Luther, *Object Lessons for Children*, 2315-7
Cross, Luther, *Story Sermons for Children*, 2328-9
De Jonge, Joanne, *More Object Lessons from Nature*, 3004-8
De Jonge, Joanne, *Object Lessons from Nature*, 2989-9
Edstrom, Lois, *Contemporary Object Lessons for Children's Church*, 3432-9
Gebhardt, Richard, & Mark Armstrong, *Object Lessons from Science Experiments*, 3811-1
Godsey, Kyle, *Object Lessons About God*, 3841-3
Hendricks, William, & Merle Den Bleyker, *Object Lessons from Sports and Games*, 4134-1
Hendricks, William, & Merle Den Bleyker, *Object Lessons That Teach Bible Truths*, 4172-4
Loeks, Mary, *Object Lessons for Children's Worship*, 5584-9
McDonald, Roderick, *Successful Object Sermons*, 6270-5
Runk, Wesley, *Object Lessons from the Bible*, 7698-6
Squyres, Greg, *Simple Object Lessons for Young Children*, 8330-3
Sullivan, Jessie, *Object Lessons and Stories for Children's Church*, 8037-1
Sullivan, Jessie, *Object Lessons with Easy-to-Find Objects*, 8190-4
Trull, Joe, *40 Object Sermons for Children*, 8831-3

# SIMPLE OBJECT LESSONS FOR YOUNG CHILDREN

**GREG SQUYRES**

 **BAKER BOOK HOUSE**
Grand Rapids, Michigan 49516

Copyright © 1992 by
Baker Book House Company
P. O. Box 6287
Grand Rapids, MI 49516-6287
All rights reserved

ISBN: 0-8010-8330-3

Printed in the United States of America

# Contents

# 1

## God Is Always There

**Preparation:** Obtain a telephone-answering machine with an outgoing message previously recorded.

**Key Verse:** I love the LORD, for he heard my voice (Ps. 116:1a).

Today I have with me a telephone-answering machine. Can anyone tell me what a machine like this is used for? *(Allow responses.)* That's right; this machine answers my phone if I'm not at home. The person calling my house can leave a message on the machine. When I return home I'll get the message to call that person back. If I could be at home all the time, I wouldn't need a machine like this. But since I can't, an answering machine comes in handy.

If you called my house and I was not at home, this is what you would hear. *(Play the outgoing message.)*

Do you think God needs an answering machine? *(Allow responses.)* God doesn't need a machine like this, because God is always available for us. No matter when we want to talk to God—day or night—God is there. God likes to hear from us. All we have to do is pray to him. It is wonderful that God is never too busy to listen to us. Let's talk with him right now.

*Prayer:* Dear God, we thank you that you love us and that you are always there for us. Amen.

# 2

# Controlling Our Anger

**Preparation:** Obtain three balloons and a bucket. Set the bucket (to be used as a goal) about fifteen feet from you and the children. You will be blowing up the balloons and trying to make them fly into the bucket.

**Key Verse:** Everyone should be quick to listen, slow to speak and slow to become angry (James 1:19b).

We're going to try to do something with these balloons and the bucket I have placed over there. I'm going to blow up these balloons one at a time and let them fly into the bucket. Let's do the first one. *(Blow up the balloon, hold it by the stem, point it toward the bucket, and then let it go. It should fly wildly and probably not go in the bucket.)* That one didn't do so well, did it? It didn't even go near the bucket. Maybe it was a bad balloon. Let's try another one. *(Repeat the process with another balloon.)* That one didn't go in the bucket either. Let's try one more. *(Repeat the process one final time.)*

Do you know what I have decided? We have no control over where the balloon flies. When we let it go, it flies crazy and wild, but doesn't go where we want it to go.

There are many happenings over which we have no control. We have no control over when the sun rises and sets. We have no control over whether or not it will rain. We can't control how hot or cold the day will be.

The Bible says there are some things that we *can* control. One of those is our anger. The Bible tells us that we should learn to control our anger, just as God controls his anger.

There are many things in life over which we have no control. We shouldn't worry about them. But we *can* control our anger, and we should work very hard to do so.

*Prayer:* Dear God, we thank you that you control your anger. Help us to learn to control ours, too. Amen.

# 3

## Telling Others About Jesus

**Preparation:** Obtain an apple, a knife, and a cutting board.

**Key Verse:** Others, like seed sown on good soil, hear the word, accept it, and produce a crop—thirty, sixty or even a hundred times what was sown (Mark 4:20).

4:15

Do you like apples? *(Allow responses.)* Which apples do you like best, the red ones or the green ones? *(Allow responses.)* Apples taste good, and they are good for us.

Have you ever looked inside an apple? *(Allow responses.)* We're going to cut this apple in half and take a look. *(Cut the apple in half and show the children the seeds.)* These are apple seeds. What are these seeds used for? *(Allow responses.)* If we plant a seed, a new apple tree will grow. The new apple tree can make more apples.

Now, let's pretend that you like apples very much and want an apple tree of your own. You have apple seeds that you can plant, but you don't want to be bothered digging in the dirt to plant the seeds. Instead, you wish very hard for an apple tree to grow. Is that a good way to make an apple tree? *(Allow responses.)*

Jesus told a story about planting seeds. He said that planting seeds is much like telling other people about him. If we want to grow an apple tree, we must plant an apple seed. And if we want others to know about Jesus, we must tell them about Jesus. Just as wishing won't make an apple tree grow, so hoping that others learn about Jesus without telling them won't make it happen.

A farmer plants seeds to grow crops. If he doesn't plant seeds, crops won't grow. Our job is to tell others about Jesus. If we don't tell them, they won't know about him.

*Prayer:* Dear God, thank you for apples and thank you for Jesus. Help us as we tell others about him. Amen.

# 4

## Run the Good Race

**Preparation:** Obtain a pair of women's running shoes and a pair of women's high-heeled dress shoes.

**Key Verse:** I have fought the good fight, I have finished the race, I have kept the faith (2 Tim. 4:7).

I have two pairs of shoes with me. Each pair has a different purpose. You can help me decide what each pair is used for.

Let's pretend a woman was going to get married. It would be a very special day for her. She would wear a fancy dress, style her hair, and be very beautiful. What pair of shoes do you think she would wear for the wedding? *(Allow responses.)* Yes, these shoes are called *dress shoes*. We wear dress shoes with fancier clothes.

Let's pretend a woman was going to run in a race. She might wear a sweatsuit or shorts for the race. Which pair of shoes do you think she would wear? *(Allow responses.)* Why would she wear these shoes? *(Allow responses.)*

These shoes *(Hold up the running shoes.)* are called *running shoes*. They are made to help a person run faster.

If an athlete was going to run a race, he or she would wear shoes like this to help him or her run a better race.

The Bible says that living for Jesus is like running a race. Let me tell you what the Bible means by that. Just as a runner in a race does his or her best, so we are to do our best to live for Jesus. If a runner stops halfway to the finish line, he or she will not finish the race. He must run the race all the way to the end. In the same way, all of our life is to be lived for Jesus. Also a runner will make preparations to help him or her run the best race he can. He will exercise and wear running shoes like these. We can do things, too, that help us to live for Jesus. Wearing running shoes won't help us live for Jesus, will it? But praying, reading the Bible, and going to Sunday school and church will.

Just as an athlete does his or her best to run a race, so we should do our best to live for Jesus.

*Prayer:* Dear God, help us to live for you each day. May we always give our best to you. Amen.

# 5

## Asking God

**Preparation:** Fill a glass with water.

**Key Verse:** Ask and it will be given to you; seek and you will find; knock and the door will be opened to you (Matt. 7:7).

I have with me a glass filled with water. When I was a little boy, my mother and father would tuck me in at bedtime; then they would leave my room so I could fall asleep. Sometimes I would lie in my bed and think, "I sure am thirsty. Boy, could I use a drink!" And so I would call out, "Mom! I'm thirsty. May I have a glass of water?" Usually, Mom would let me get up for a drink, and then I would go back to bed.

Now, suppose I was lying in my bed thirsty, but I didn't ask my mother for a drink. I wished I could have a drink; I was getting more and more thirsty—but I wouldn't ask for water. If I didn't ask for a drink, I wouldn't get a drink, would I?

The Bible says that God listens to us, and that we can ask him for things, too. That doesn't mean God will give us whatever we ask for. What if you were in bed and you called out to your mother, "Mom, may I have a candy bar?" What do you think your mother would say? *(Allow responses.)* She probably would say *no!* A candy bar would not be good for you at bedtime. In the same way God will give us only that which is good for us. We may wonder sometimes why God doesn't always give us what we ask for, but he knows better than anyone else what would be good for us and what would not. God has promised to give us everything we need, but he may not give us everything we want.

When we talk to God, we should not be selfish or ask for something that would not be pleasing to him. One wonderful thing we can ask for is that God will help people in need. God is pleased when we make requests like that.

So when we talk to God, we can ask him for good things. We know he hears us, and he will give us what we need.

*Prayer:* Dear God, thank you for listening to us and for giving us what we need. Amen.

# 6

# The Bible Is a Book to Read

**Preparation:** Obtain a Bible, a dictionary, and a phone book.

**Key Verse:** Devote yourself to the public reading of Scripture, to preaching and to teaching (1 Tim. 4:13b).

I have three books with me today. Each book has a purpose. Let's talk about each one.

First, I have a phone book. What is a phone book used for? *(Allow responses.)* That's right. A phone book is used to find phone numbers of people we want to call on the telephone. Do you ever read the phone book just for fun, or have your mom or dad read it to you at bedtime? *(Allow responses.)* We don't read the phone book for fun. We read it when we need to know a certain phone number.

The second book I have is a dictionary. What is a dictionary used for? *(Allow responses.)* A dictionary tells us the meaning of words we don't know, and helps us to spell big words. Do you enjoy listening to someone read from the dictionary? *(Allow responses.)* Dictionaries don't have stories in them. We don't read from a dictionary at bedtime. We read a dictionary to learn about words.

The last book I have is a Bible. The Bible is different from the dictionary and the phone book. First, it is different because it is God's Word to us. Phone books and dictionaries are written by people, but the Bible is God's Book.

But there is another reason that the Bible is different. We read a dictionary or a phone book when we need to know about a word or a phone number. We don't read those books just because we enjoy reading them and find them interesting. We call books like these *reference books*. But the Bible is not a reference book. We read the Bible because it has interesting stories, important lessons, and because we enjoy reading it. We don't read the Bible only when we want to look up something. We read the Bible every day because we can learn about God and it is God's Word to us.

*Prayer:* Thank you, God, for the Bible. Thank you that as we read the Bible, we learn more about you. Amen.

# 7

## Changed on the Inside

**Preparation:** Obtain two eggs. Hard-boil one of them, but don't peel it. Have a bowl to crack the raw egg into, and a cloth to wipe your hands with.

**Key Verse:** Therefore, if anyone is in Christ, he is a new creation; the old has gone, the new has come! (2 Cor. 5:17).

I have two eggs with me today. These eggs look much the same on the outside. They are both white. They are both about the same size and the same shape. But they are actually very different. We can't tell the difference by looking at the outside, because the difference in the eggs is on the inside. Let me show you. *(First crack the uncooked egg.)* This egg is a regular uncooked egg. How do you think the second egg will be different? *(Allow responses, then peel the hard-boiled egg.)* Although both these eggs looked very much alike on the outside, they were actually quite different on the inside. One of the eggs had been changed on the inside as I cooked it.

These two eggs show us what happens when a person accepts Jesus into his or her life. When that happens, the person's life is changed on the inside. He or she won't look much different on the outside, but don't let that fool you. A great change occurs when Jesus comes into our hearts. If we are sorry for our sins, Jesus forgives us. We think and act differently. We want to do whatever pleases Jesus. We want to tell others about Jesus. And we know that we will never die, but we will live forever with Jesus in heaven.

There is something else about accepting Jesus into our lives. *(Hold up the hard-boiled egg.)* This egg, now that it has been changed, will never be a raw egg again. It will always be a hard-boiled egg. In the same way, when we accept Jesus into our lives, the change that takes place on the inside will last forever and ever. It is wonderful to be changed on the inside when we invite Jesus into our lives.

*Prayer:* Dear God, thank you for the change that Jesus makes in our lives. And thank you that when we ask him into our lives, he is there to stay. Amen.

# 8

# The Carrot and
# the Candy Bar

**Preparation:** You will need a candy bar and a carrot.

**Key Verse:** Choose for yourselves this day whom you will serve (Josh. 24:15b).

I have two things with me today that are good to eat—a carrot and a candy bar. Suppose you had been playing outside for a long time and you became hungry. You went inside your house and said to your mother, "I sure am hungry. May I have a snack?" Your mother said to you, "Sure. Here is a carrot and a candy bar. Choose which one you would like to eat."

Well, you have a decision to make. If you had to choose between the carrot and the candy bar, which one would you choose? *(Allow responses.)*

Every day we have choices to make. You may have to choose which shirt or dress you will wear, which game you will play, or what you will eat for a snack. Sometimes choices are hard to make, but we all must learn to make decisions.

A choice all of us make every day is whether or not we will live in a way that pleases Jesus. We live for Jesus when we do good things, talk nicely, and treat other people with kindness.

Let's imagine some things that might happen, and you help me decide if they would please Jesus: *(State each situation and allow responses.)*

Cutting in line to play tetherball at school.

Obeying your mother and father.

Going to Sunday school and church.

Kicking your brother or sister.

Telling someone "thank you" when they have done something nice for you.

We make a lot of choices every day! Let's always try to make choices that make Jesus happy.

*Prayer:* Dear God, help us to do and say those things that please you. Amen.

# 9

# Everyone Is Special

**Preparation:** Obtain three sets of items that are identical except for their color. For this lesson I used two basketballs, two cups, and two towels.

**Key Verse:** There is neither Jew nor Greek, slave nor free, male nor female, for you are all one in Christ Jesus (Gal. 3:28).

I have several items we will talk about today. First, I have two basketballs. One basketball is orange, and the other is brown. Which basketball do you think is better? *(Allow responses.)* Do you think one is better than the other just because of its color? *(Allow responses.)* The important thing about a basketball is how good it bounces, not what color it is.

Let's talk about these two cups. They look the same except for one thing: their color. These cups are the same size, the same shape, and can hold the same amount of water. But their color is different. Do you think one of these cups is better than the other just because of its color? *(Allow responses.)* If the two cups can do the same job equally well, the color does not make one better than the other.

Finally let's look at these two towels. One towel is pink, and the other is blue. Do you think the pink towel is better because it is pink, or do you think the blue towel is better because it is blue? *(Allow responses.)* Actually, the important thing about a towel is how well it dries up water. The color of a towel will not make it dry any better or any worse.

God has made people a little like these objects we have talked about. People come in all colors. God made some with black skin, others with white skin. Some have brown skin, or reddish skin, or yellowish skin. But no person is better than another because of the color of skin. God made every person and loves every person. A song we sometimes sing says:

Red and yellow, black and white;
All are precious in his sight.

Everyone is special to God, no matter what color he has made them.

*Prayer:* Dear God, thank you for all the colors you have made. Thank you for making people different colors, too. Help us to love everyone the same as you do. Amen.

# 10

## The Devil Is a Deceiver

**Preparation:** Fill a drinking glass with water from a fish tank.

**Key Verse:** And the devil, who deceived them, was thrown into the lake of burning sulfur (Rev. 20:10b).

Have you ever been so thirsty that you just *had* to have a drink of water? Sometimes when we play outside on a hot day, our mouths get dry and we have to get a drink. Or sometimes when going to bed, it is hard to get to sleep unless we first get a drink of water.

Thinking about water makes us a little thirsty, doesn't it? I have a glass of water with me. Would anyone like a drink of water? *(Allow a child to volunteer.)* Before you drink the water, maybe I should tell you where it came from. The water in this glass came from my fish tank. Do you still want a drink of it? *(Allow the child to respond.)*

The water in this glass would probably not be very good for us. The water looks good, but if we were to drink it we might get sick.

The water in the glass reminds me of how the devil works. The devil is always trying to make us do, say, or believe things that look as though they would be good. But when we find out more about them, we find out that what the devil wants us to do is not good for us.

The Bible calls the devil a deceiver. A deceiver is someone who tries to fool us. The devil is always trying to fool us so we do something wrong. Do you know why the devil tries to fool us? It is because he doesn't love us. Since he doesn't love us, we cannot trust him.

But there is someone who loves us very much. Can anyone tell me who that is? (*Allow responses.*) Yes, Jesus loves us and wants the best for us. He would never trick us into doing wrong. And because he loves us so much, we can trust him.

*Prayer:* Dear God, thank you for Jesus, who loves us very much. Help us not to be fooled by the devil so we do what is wrong, but to only do what pleases you. Amen.

# 11

# A Meal to Remember (Lord's Supper)

**Preparation:** Obtain a hot dog.

**Key Verse:** Do this in remembrance of me (Luke 22:19c).

Sometimes when I am eating certain foods, I begin to think about other things. Let me tell you what I mean. This is a hot dog. Can anyone guess what I think about when I eat a hot dog? *(Allow responses.)* I think about baseball. I have gone to many major league baseball games, and whenever I go, I always go to the snack bar and get a hot dog. I put mustard, relish, ketchup, and onions on it. As I watch the game I eat my hot dog. So now, whenever I eat a hot dog, no matter where I am, I think of baseball.

Other foods that I eat remind me of something else. When I eat a turkey dinner I think of Thanksgiving. That is because I always eat turkey for Thanksgiving dinner. Whenever I eat a cherry pie, I think of my grandmother. That is because when I was a boy, my grandmother often made me a cherry pie when I went to her house. She knew cherry pie was my favorite.

Today the members in our church will be eating the Lord's Supper. Just as a hot dog, a turkey dinner, and a cherry pie remind me of something else, whenever I eat the Lord's Supper, *it* reminds me of something else. When Jesus first ate the Lord's Supper with his disciples, he said that whenever we eat it we are to remember him. So, whenever I eat the Lord's Supper, I think of Jesus and how much he loves me. That's why we eat the Lord's Supper—it reminds us of Jesus.

*Prayer:* Dear God, thank you for Jesus and his love for us. Help us to remember him every day. Amen.

# 12

## The Happiest Easter
## (Easter)

**Preparation:** Obtain an Easter basket filled with candy.

**Key Verse:** He has risen, just as he said (Matt. 28:6b).

Easter has always been a happy day for me. When I was a little boy, I would get up early on Easter morning and sneak into our family room. There I would find one of these *(hold up Easter basket)*—an Easter basket filled with candy just for me. As you can imagine, my discovery of the Easter basket made me very happy because I liked the candy.

As happy as I used to get when I discovered my Easter basket, my happiness couldn't come close to what some women felt on an Easter morning about two thousand years ago. These women didn't discover an Easter basket that morning. They discovered something that would make them happier than any Easter basket ever could. Can anybody tell me what these women discovered? *(Allow responses.)* That's right. They discovered the empty tomb of Jesus.

Jesus was a friend of these women, so when he died they were very sad. After a couple days they went to the place where Jesus was buried. They loved Jesus very much and wanted to visit his grave. But when they came to his grave, Jesus wasn't there! An angel stood by the grave and told them Jesus had come back to life. He wasn't dead. Jesus was alive!

This was a happy day for these women. They were excited about this good news, and they hurried to tell Jesus' other friends. The day that Jesus came back to life was the first Easter. As happy as we may be about Easter baskets filled with candy, we should be happiest that Jesus came back to life. He lives today, and he'll live forever!

*Prayer:* Dear God, we are happy that Jesus came back to life on the first Easter morning. Help us to tell others that Jesus is the reason that Easter is special. Amen.

# 13

## Faith in God

**Preparation:** Place a flower in a shoe box. Cover the box with a lid.

**Key Verse:** Now faith is being sure of what we hope for and certain of what we do not see (Heb. 11:1).

Do you know what I have inside this box? It is a pretty flower. I'm going to let one other person see the flower—but nobody else. The rest of you will have to believe there really is a flower in the box. *(Select a child to peek into the box.)*

*(Ask the child the following questions:)* Did you see anything in the box? What did you see? What color was it?

*(Ask the other children:)* How many of you believe there is a flower in the box? *(Allow responses.)* Although you don't see it, most [or all] of you believe that there is a flower in the box.

There is a word for believing in something you can't see. It is called *faith*. When people say they have faith in God, what they mean is that even though they can't see God with their eyes, they still believe in him. The flower in this box is a real flower, and we can believe it is in the box even though we can't see it. In the same way, God is real, and we can believe in him even though we can't see him.

God loves us, and even though we can't see him, he sees us and does wonderful things for us. Let's pray to him and thank him for his goodness.

*Prayer:* Dear God, thank you that even though we can't see you, we can have faith in you, knowing that you love us and care for us. Amen.

# 14

# A Cheerful Giver

**Preparation:** Obtain one of the offering plates your church uses.

**Key Verse:** God loves a cheerful giver (2 Cor. 9:7c).

This is an object we use every Sunday in our church. It is called an *offering plate.* Can anyone tell me what an offering plate is used for? *(Allow responses.)* Every Sunday there is a special time in the service when people can give some of their money. These plates are passed down all the rows where people are sitting, and people put into the plates the money they want to give.

Do you know where the money goes after that? It helps to pay for things our church needs, like Sunday school books and music. Part of the money pays the pastor and other helpers in the church. Some of the money helps poor people who live in our town and some pays for missionaries in countries all over the world. In other words the money we give in the offering does God's work in our church, our town, and around the world.

Should giving some of our money for the offering make us sad or happy? *(Allow responses.)* It should make us happy because it is used to do so much good. We also should be happy about giving because the Bible says, "God loves a cheerful giver." It makes God happy when we give an offering cheerfully.

Everybody—both children and grown-ups—can help the church do God's work as they give some of their money at offering time.

*Prayer:* Thank you, God, that our money can be used in many wonderful ways through our church. Help us to be cheerful givers. Amen.

# 15

## God Is Everlasting

**Preparation:** Mark a calendar with several birth dates.

**Key Verse:** Before the mountains were born
or you brought forth the earth and the world,
from everlasting to everlasting you are God
(Ps. 90:2).

I like birthdays, don't you? *(Allow responses.)* I have a calendar that tells me when some of my friends' birthdays are. Let's look at the calendar. *(Show several birth dates that you have marked.)*

Do you know when your birthday is? *(Allow responses. Let several of the children share their date.)*

Everybody has a birthday, and birthdays are special days. There is one birthday that we can't mark on our calendar. Do you know whose birthday that might be? *(Allow responses.)* We can't mark God's birthday on our calendar, because God doesn't have a birthday.

A birthday is a celebration of the day we were born. God doesn't have a birthday because God was never born. The Bible says, "From everlasting to everlasting you are God." That means that God always has been and always will be. He was never born, because he has always existed. And God will never die.

God is not sad about not having a birthday. I think he enjoys celebrating all of our birthdays with us, because God knows and loves everybody. And since God is everlasting, he will always be there for us, forever and ever.

*Prayer:* God, you are so great, for you existed before anything else. Thank you for always being there for us, forever and ever. Amen.

# 16

## God's Love Never Expires

**Preparation:** Obtain a driver's license.

**Key Verse:** Never will I leave you;
never will I forsake you (Heb. 13:5b).

I have with me today my driver's license. Does anyone know what a driver's license is for? *(Allow responses.)* My driver's license allows me to drive my car. I had to take a test to receive my license. After I took the test and received my license, I was allowed to drive on the roads.

There is a word on my license I want you to notice. It is the word *expires. (Point it out on the license.)* Do you know what *expires* means? *(Allow responses.) Expires* means that after a certain date, my license isn't good anymore. My license expires in the year _____. To be able to drive after that date, I must renew my license. So this isn't good forever. I will have to renew my license and perhaps take tests.

Driver's licenses are not the only things that expire. Medicines expire. After a certain amount of time, they are no longer any good. Food expires. When you buy milk, the carton has a date printed on it which tells how long it will be good. Did you ever drink milk that was not good? *(Allow responses.)*

Yes, many things don't last forever. But the Bible gives us a wonderful promise about something that does last forever. In the Bible God says, "Never will I leave you; never will I forsake you." That means that God is always there for us. When we accept Jesus into our hearts, Jesus is there to stay. He will never leave. We don't have to accept Jesus again and again. Accepting Jesus is not like a driver's license that doesn't last forever. Jesus will never leave us. His love for us never expires.

*Prayer:* Dear Lord, thank you for your love for us that lasts forever. Thank you for never leaving us. Amen.

# 17

## Growing and Learning

**Preparation:** Obtain a baby bottle, some baby clothes, and a jar of baby food.

**Key Verse:** Like newborn babies, crave pure spiritual milk, so that by it you may grow up in your salvation (1 Peter 2:2).

*Show the baby bottle.)* When you have been outside playing hard and you begin to feel hungry, you probably come inside your house, open the refrigerator door and take out one of these to snack on, don't you? *(Allow responses.)* You don't really drink from a baby bottle anymore, because you have grown up, and baby bottles are for babies. Do you eat this kind of food? *(Show baby food; allow responses.)* No, this baby food is for babies, too. And what about when you get dressed in the morning, do you wear clothes that look like this? *(Show baby clothes; allow responses.)* No, these are all baby things. Now that we have grown, we don't use baby things any longer.

Growing up means that our bodies get bigger, taller, and stronger. It also means that we learn new subjects.

We go to school to learn to read, and write, and learn about our world. We also need to learn new facts about God. When we come to Sunday school and church and read our Bibles, we can learn more about God. As we learn more about God, he becomes more special to us.

The Bible says that a person who grows up but doesn't learn new facts about God is like a grown-up person who still drinks from a baby bottle. And so it is important that as we grow up, we also learn. We should learn new facts about our world, but we should also learn something new about God every day.

*Prayer:* Dear God, thank you for being our special friend. As we grow, help us to always be learning something new about you. Amen.

# 18

## No Glasses in Heaven

**Preparation:** Obtain a pair of eyeglasses.

**Key Verses:** But our citizenship is in heaven. And we eagerly await a Savior from there, the Lord Jesus Christ, who, by the power that enables him to bring everything under his control, will transform our lowly bodies so that they will be like his glorious body (Phil. 3:20–21).

I have with me a pair of eyeglasses. Many people have to wear eyeglasses or contact lenses to see better. Without glasses everything would look fuzzy or blurred, but with glasses, everything clears up.

These glasses remind me of something I was thinking about recently. People who wear glasses need them to see better. They have their eyes checked often to make sure their glasses are strong enough. Sometimes they need new glasses, because their eyes have become a little weaker. Some people will always have to wear glasses to see well.

I began thinking about heaven. I wondered if there will be any eye doctors in heaven so people can have their eyes checked and get glasses when they need them. What do you think? *(Allow responses.)*

I am sure there will be some eye doctors in heaven—but they won't be checking people's eyes to see if they need glasses! When we get to heaven, our bodies will be perfect. People who cannot see well now will be able to see perfectly in heaven. There won't be any need for glasses in heaven, because everyone's eyes will be perfect. Even people who are blind will be able to see when they get to heaven.

Heaven is a great place. We can thank God for heaven. It is a place of perfect happiness.

*Prayer:* Dear God, we thank you for glasses we can wear to see better. But we thank you that when we get to heaven we won't need them, because heaven is a perfect place. Thank you for the perfect happiness of heaven. Amen.

# 19

## It's What Is Inside That Counts

**Preparation:** Dye several Easter eggs.

**Key Verse:** So God created man in his own image, in the image of God he created him; male and female he created them (Gen. 1:27).

Today I have several Easter eggs. Have you ever gone on an Easter egg hunt? It is fun to search for the eggs and see how many you can find.

*(Choose one child and ask:)* Of all the Easter eggs I have with me, which do you think is the prettiest? *(Hold it up and say:)* Why did you choose this egg? *(Allow him/her to explain.)*

Now, let me ask you another question. Out of all the eggs I have with me, which one do you think tastes the best? *(Allow responses.)* We can't tell which one tastes the best by looking at the outside, can we? In fact, no matter what color the Easter eggs are on the outside, they are all the same on the inside, aren't they? They all taste the same, no matter what they look like on the outside.

We can learn a lesson from the Easter eggs. The Bible says that God made every man, woman, boy, and girl. Some he made tall, some he made short. Some he gave blond hair, others he gave black hair. Some he gave brown skin, some white skin, and others black skin. But just like the Easter eggs, it doesn't really matter what's on the outside. It's what is inside that counts. On the outside we may have different color hair or skin, but on the inside we are all the same. God made every one of us, and it doesn't make any difference to him what we look like on the outside, because he knows what is on the inside. God loves everybody the same, and he wants us to love others that way too.

*Prayer:* Dear God, thank you for making us and loving us. Help us to love others, too. Amen.

# 20

## Dads Aren't Perfect
## (Father's Day)

**Preparation:** Obtain a chipped cup or dish.

**Key Verse:** For all have sinned and fall short of the glory of God (Rom. 3:23).

I have a cup with me today. It is a pretty cup. But when we look very closely at the cup we discover something about it. What do you discover when you look closely at the cup? *(Allow children to examine the cup and respond to the question.)* This is a very pretty cup, but when we look closely we discover it has a chip in it. And so the cup is not perfect, because it has a chip in it.

Fathers are a little like this cup. Just as this cup is not perfect, fathers are not perfect either. Of all the fathers in all the world, not one is perfect in every way.

Fathers can be great people, especially when they spend time with us. But the Bible says that nobody is completely perfect, and that includes fathers. So sometimes fathers say words they shouldn't say or do things they shouldn't do. That shows that they are not perfect.

So remember that fathers are a little like this cup. They aren't perfect. And when they say something they shouldn't say or do something they shouldn't do, they need our love and forgiveness.

*Prayer:* Thank you, God, for fathers. Help us to love them at all times. Amen.

# 21

## People Are Made Like God

**Preparation:** Obtain a crystal goblet and a paper cup.

**Key Verse:** So God created man in his own image,
in the image of God he created him;
male and female he created them (Gen. 1:27).

I am holding two items—a crystal goblet that cost a lot of money and a paper cup. These items are alike in some ways. Both the goblet and the paper cup can hold water or punch or something else that we could drink. But they are also different. The goblet costs a lot more than the paper cup. It is much fancier. Also, it will last much longer than a paper cup.

Now let's pretend that paper cups can think. We know they really can't, but suppose this paper cup saw the fancy crystal goblet and thought to himself, *I'm just as good as that goblet. I can hold water. I'm just as pretty. In every way I'm just as good if not better than the goblet.* Wouldn't that be a silly thought? Anybody can tell that the goblet is much greater in value than the paper cup.

Our friendship with God is somewhat like the goblet and the paper cup. The Bible says that God made us in his image. That means we are like God. We know that God is love and he is kind and fair. Since we are made in his image, we are to be loving, kind, and fair too.

However, just because we are *like* God, it doesn't mean we *are* a god. Just as it was silly for the paper cup to think he was in every way as good as the crystal goblet, it is also silly for people to think they are as good as God. There is only one God, and he is greater than any man or woman, boy or girl.

Although nobody is as great as God, we can be thankful that he has made us a little like him. God loves us and we can be like him as we are kind and loving to others.

*Prayer:* Dear God, thank you for loving us and making us a little like you. Help us to be more like you every day as we love others. Amen.

# 22

## More Like Jesus

**Preparation:** Obtain a basketball.

**Key Verse:** And we pray this in order that you may live a life worthy of the Lord and may please him in every way (Col. 1:10a).

This is a basketball. Do any of you like to play basketball? *(Allow responses.)* Have you ever seen a basketball game? *(Allow responses.)*

When you play basketball, you take the ball and throw it into a metal ring called the hoop. Every time the ball goes through the hoop, your team gets two points. The goal then is to do your best to throw the ball through the hoop. The more times you throw it through the hoop, the more points your team gets.

A goal is something we try our best to do. The goal in basketball is throwing the ball through the hoop. But there are other kinds of goals we have. Maybe your goal is to do well in school; or your goal may be to keep your room clean or to eat your vegetables at dinner every night.

It is good to have goals, things we are trying our best to do. One goal we all should have is to be more like Jesus. He was always kind and helpful to others. Let's make that one of our goals. Let's ask God to help us reach our goal of being more like Jesus.

*Prayer:* Dear God, thank you for Jesus and his love. Help us to be more like him every day. Amen.

# 23

## Growing to Be Like Jesus

**Preparation:** Obtain a picture of you as a child.

**Key Verse:**  But grow in the grace and knowledge of our
Lord and Savior Jesus Christ (2 Peter 3:18a).

Today I have a picture with me. It is a picture
of someone you know. Look carefully at this picture
and tell me if you know this person. *(Allow the children
to look at the picture and try to guess who it is.)*

The picture I am showing you is a picture of me. It
doesn't look very much like me, does it? It was taken
many years ago, before any of you were born. It shows
what I looked like when I was a child.

I look different today because I have grown a lot
since this picture was taken. Something would be
wrong if I looked like the child in this picture for the
rest of my life. As I grow, I am supposed to look different. As each of you becomes a grown-up, you also will
look different from what you do today.

Growing is an important part of life. Not only are
our bodies supposed to grow, but we are to grow in
another way also. The Bible says we are to "grow in the

grace and knowledge of our Lord and Savior Jesus Christ." That means we are to grow to be more like Jesus.

There are many things we know about Jesus. Jesus was kind. He loved people. He respected others. He honored his mother and father. To grow to be like Jesus means we want to live like Jesus. We want to be kind and loving and respectful. Let's do our best to live like Jesus today, so that we can grow to be more and more like him in the days and years to come.

*Prayer:* Father, help us to live like Jesus lived. Help us to be kind and loving to others. Amen.

# 24

# Whom Does God Love Best?

**Preparation:** Obtain a world globe.

**Key Verse:** For God so loved the world that he gave his one and only Son, that whoever believes in him shall not perish but have eternal life (John 3:16).

This is a globe. A globe is a round map of the earth. A globe shows all the oceans on the earth as well as all the land on the earth where people live.

Let's look carefully at the globe today. I have something I want you to help me decide. I want you to tell me who in the world God loves best.

Here is a boot-shaped country called Italy. Do you think God loves the people of Italy? Next to Italy is France. (A new Disney World just opened there.) Whom do you think God loves the most: the people in Italy or France? *(Allow responses.)* Near France is Germany, and over here is South Africa. Across the ocean is the United States of America. Let's see, we've mentioned Italy,

France, Germany, South Africa, and the United States. Which country do you think God loves the most?

The answer to our question is found in the Bible. John 3:16 says, "For God so loved the world that he gave his one and only Son, that whoever believes in him shall not perish but have eternal life."

"For God so loved the world. . . ." God doesn't love Italy more than France, or the United States more than South Africa. God loves the whole world. He loves everybody just the same. And it is because God loves the whole world that Jesus came, so that whoever believes in him will receive eternal life.

*Prayer:* Thank you, God, for loving us and sending your Son, Jesus, into the world. Amen.

# 25

## Loving All People

**Preparation:** Obtain a cherry pie.

**Key Verse:** Let us love one another (1 John 4:7a).

Do you love pies? *(Allow responses.)* I love pies—especially this kind of pie. This is a cherry pie. It has been a favorite of mine for as long as I can remember. When I was a little boy and my grandmother wanted to do something special for me, she would often make me a cherry pie.

Why do you love pies? *(Allow responses.)* Most of us love pies because we like how they taste. When we put a piece of pie in our mouths, it makes us feel good so we love it.

Do you love people? *(Allow responses.)* We all love people. The Bible tells us to love people. It says, "Let us love one another." But do we love one another in the same way that we love a cherry pie? *(Allow responses.)* Loving a pie is easy to do. It tastes good and makes us feel good. Loving people is sometimes harder. Sometimes people aren't nice to us. They may do or say mean things to hurt our feelings. When that happens, we don't feel good about them.

So when the Bible says to "love one another," it is telling us to do something that is sometimes hard to do. But Jesus loved everybody, even people who were mean to him. And although it is very hard to do, Jesus wants us to love everyone too.

We can't love only people who make us feel good or do nice things for us, can we? Loving people isn't the same as loving pies. Loving some people is hard to do, but we must try if we want to be more like Jesus.

*Prayer:* Dear God, help us to love all people. Thank you for loving us. Amen.

# 26

## One God Is Enough

**Preparation:** Obtain an umbrella, an apple, and a shoe.

**Key Verse:** The Lord our God, the Lord is one (Mark 12:29b).

I have three items: an umbrella, an apple, and a shoe. Let's talk about them one at a time. First let's talk about the umbrella.

Let's pretend that when church was over today it began to rain. It didn't just trickle. It rained hard—harder than it has rained in years. Nobody wanted to get out in the rain, because they didn't want to get wet. But one person had an umbrella. Everybody in the church decided that they would crowd under the umbrella together to try to stay dry in the rain. Do you think we all would stay dry? (*Allow responses.*) All of us could not possibly fit under one umbrella. In a heavy rain one umbrella is not enough for everybody, is it?

Let's pretend now that everybody in our church was very hungry. It had been hours and hours since we had eaten, and we needed something to eat soon. We started looking around the church for something to eat, and in the kitchen we found one apple. We decided that everyone in church would take one bite out of the apple. Do you think this apple would be big enough to feed everybody? *(Allow responses.)* One apple is not enough to feed many hungry people, is it?

Now let's pretend that you were getting dressed in the morning. You put on your pants and shirt or your dress, and then you went to look for shoes to wear. As you searched your closet, you found only one shoe. Do you think that one shoe would be enough? *(Allow responses.)* One shoe would not be enough, because we have two feet, don't we?

There are many times when one of something isn't enough. But now let's pretend once more. Let's pretend that you had a problem. You had thought and thought about what to do, but you couldn't solve the problem by yourself. You needed help, and so you decided to pray about it. How many gods would you have to pray to about your problem? *(Allow responses.)* You would pray to only one God about your problem, because in all of the world, there is only one true God. And do you know what? One umbrella may not be enough, one apple may not be enough, and one shoe certainly is not enough. *But one God is all we need!* He is big enough and strong enough and loving enough to handle all the problems in the world.

*Prayer:* Dear God, we thank you that you are the only God in all the world, and that you are all we need. Help us to trust in you with our problems. Amen.

# 27

## Being Patient

**Preparation:** Buy two bottles of ketchup. Empty one halfway. Obtain a large bowl and a measuring cup filled with water.

**Key Verse:** Be completely humble and gentle; be patient, bearing with one another in love (Eph. 4:2).

*H*old up the filled ketchup bottle.) How many of you like ketchup? *(Allow responses.)* I like ketchup. I eat it on hamburgers, french fries, meat loaf, and other things. Today we're going to do something with this bottle of ketchup. I need a volunteer. *(Get a volunteer. Instruct him or her to begin pouring the ketchup from the bottle into the large bowl. Don't let the child shake it or pound on it. Just have him or her turn it upside down and wait.)* It sure takes a long time for ketchup to come out of a bottle, doesn't it? Ketchup is very slow.

I have an idea. Let's try to make the ketchup pour out faster. *(Have the volunteer put down the bottle of ketchup. Get the half-filled bottle and the measuring cup of water. As you are talking, pour the water into the ketchup bottle, and then shake it to mix.)* I'm going to pour some water into this bottle of ketchup, and then mix it up. Then we will see if it pours out faster. *(After mixing the ketchup with the water, hand it to the volunteer to pour into the bowl. It will come out quickly.)*

That ketchup came out fast, didn't it? If you had the choice, would you choose the fast ketchup, or the slow ketchup? *(Allow responses.)* Most of you would choose the slow ketchup.

The ketchup has taught us something. Faster isn't always better. Sometimes we have to be patient to get what is best.

We may at times get impatient with friends, brothers or sisters, moms or dads, or other people. We may even get impatient with God. When we pray, we may feel God doesn't answer our prayer fast enough.

But, remember the ketchup; fast isn't always best. If we are patient, God can give us what is best for us at the best time.

And another point about being patient: The Bible says that God is patient with us. And so as we try to be more like God, we should do our best to be patient.

*Prayer:* Dear God, thank you for always being patient with us. Help us to be patient, too. Amen.

# 28

## Our Prayer List

**Preparation:** Prepare three lists. List THINGS TO DO TODAY, a grocery list, and a Christmas WISH LIST.

**Key Verse:** Pray also for me (Eph. 6:19a).

Today I have three lists. We make lists to help us remember. Many times I would have forgotten important matters if I had not written them down on a list.

We're going to play a game with my lists. There are many different kinds of lists. I'm going to read you the items on each of my lists, and you try to guess what kind of list it is.

My first list has these:

| | |
|---|---|
| feed the dog | read the Bible |
| do my homework | clean my room |

Can anyone tell me what kind of list that is? (*Allow responses.*) That is a list of what I have to do today. Let me read you my second list, and you try to guess what kind of list it is:

| | |
|---|---|
| tomatoes | bread |
| cereal | spaghetti noodles |
| milk | |

What kind of list is that? *(Allow responses.)* That was a grocery list. Now let's try one more. Here is my last list:

| | |
|---|---|
| stuffed animal | train set |
| basketball | crayons |
| fire engine | |

What do you think that list is? *(Allow responses.)* That is a Christmas wish list. I'm sure you have your own Christmas list. Lists remind us of what is important to us.

There is one other kind of list I want to talk about. It is called a *prayer list.* When we pray, we want to remember to pray for people we love or who need God's help. Who should be on our prayer list? *(Allow responses. If needed, you may help them by suggesting people for the list, such as pastor, mother and father, people who need food, teacher, and so forth. As people are mentioned, write their names on a piece of paper.)*

We've made a good prayer list. Let me read it to you. *(Read it.)* This list will help us remember those to pray for. You may want to make your own prayer list at home. For now, let's pray for the people who are on this list.

*Prayer:* Dear God, we pray for all the people on our prayer list. *(Recall some by name.)* Help us to remember to pray for others. Amen.

# 29

# In Remembrance of Me (Lord's Supper)

**Preparation:** Be prepared to show a photograph of some significant person from your life who has died. (In this lesson I refer to my grandfather.)

**Key Verse:** Do this in remembrance of me (1 Cor. 11:24c).

I have a picture I would like to show you. This is a picture of my grandfather. As I look at this picture, I remember a lot about my grandfather. He loved to tell jokes and laugh. He liked to go to church and sing songs about Jesus. I remember times we talked, and many things we did together. I no longer have my grandfather with me, because he is now in heaven. Someday I know I will see him again. But until I see him in heaven, it is good to look at this photograph and remember. Memories are wonderful.

Today our church members will be taking the Lord's Supper. The main reason that Jesus told us to take the Lord's Supper is so that we will remember him. There are many facts we remember about Jesus. You may have a favorite story about Jesus. Maybe your favorite story is the one that tells about Jesus' birth, or the story of Jesus feeding the huge crowd of people with only five loaves of bread and two fish, or the story of Jesus telling Zacchaeus to come down from the tree because he wanted to go to his house with him. Some of you have invited Jesus into your lives as Savior, and you can remember the day that happened. You may remember a sad day that Jesus helped you through. Those are special memories.

Jesus is now gone into heaven. Someday we will see him, but for now, we can remember him. And so, as our members take the Lord's Supper today, be thinking about the ways Jesus is special to you. We take the Lord's Supper to remember Jesus.

*Prayer:* Dear God, thank you for our memories and for all the ways Jesus is special to us. Amen.

# 30

## God Gives Good Things

**Preparation:** Empty a cereal box. Pour enough gravel in the box to fill a cereal bowl. Have the box of gravel, the bowl, a spoon, and milk available for the lesson.

**Key Verses:** Which of you, if his son asks for bread, will give him a stone? . . . If you, then, though you are evil, know how to give good gifts to your children, how much more will your Father in heaven give good gifts to those who ask him! (Matt. 7:9, 11).

How many of you had breakfast this morning? *(Allow responses.)* Perhaps one of you is still a little hungry. I have something here you can eat. *(Show the cereal box.)* Do you like cereal? *(Allow responses.)* Do you like it better with milk or right out of the box? *(Allow responses.)* Let's pour some into the bowl and add some milk. *(Pour the gravel into the bowl and add milk.)*

Who would like to eat some? *(Allow responses.)* What is wrong? *(Allow responses.)* Probably none of you had a breakfast like this. These are rocks in this bowl. Nobody eats rocks for breakfast. But what about when you come home from school and want a snack? When you ask your mom for something good to eat, doesn't she give you a rock or two to munch on? *(Allow responses.)* Well, at dinnertime, don't you ever eat rock loaf? *(Allow responses.)*

It is silly to think about eating rocks, isn't it? If you asked your mom or dad for something good to eat, they would give you some bread or an apple or something else that is good for you. They wouldn't give you a rock.

One day Jesus was teaching about eating rocks. He said that just as our moms or dads wouldn't give us a rock to eat, because it is bad for us, so God, our heavenly Father, will not give us anything bad. Our mothers and fathers want the best for us. In the same way God loves us and wants the best for us, and gives us whatever is for our good.

*Prayer:* Dear God, thank you for loving us and for giving us what is good for us. Amen.

# 31

## Rules to Live By

**Preparation:** Obtain a baseball bat, ball, and glove.

**Key Verse:** Be careful to follow every command I am giving you today (Deut. 8:1a).

Today I have some equipment used to play baseball. First I have a baseball. It would be impossible to play baseball without a baseball, wouldn't it? Next I have a glove. We catch the baseball using the glove. And finally I have a bat. We hit the ball with the baseball bat.

Have any of you ever played baseball? *(Allow responses.)* Baseball is fun to play, but we have to play by the rules. Baseball has many rules. Can anyone tell me a rule of baseball? *(Allow responses. If necessary, remind them of some of the rules, such as "three strikes make an out"; "after hitting the ball, a player runs to first, second, third, and then home, in that order"; "if a player on the other team tags you with the ball, you are out"; "the team with the most runs at the end of the game wins.")*

Let's imagine that two teams are playing baseball, but one of the teams doesn't want to play by the rules.

They want five outs instead of three, and they don't want to have to run to all of the bases, only to first and then home. Do you think that the game would be much fun? *(Allow responses.)* The game would not be fun if the teams that were playing did not follow the rules.

God has given us some rules to live by. Can anyone tell me one of God's rules? *(Allow responses.)* Some of the rules are that we are not to steal; we aren't to lie; and we are to honor our fathers and mothers. Just as rules are needed in a baseball game, rules are also needed in life. If baseball teams don't play by the rules, the game is not fun. And if we do not live by the rules God has given us, life is not fun. God gives us rules to make life better. Life can be fun as we obey God's rules.

*Prayer:* Dear God, help us to live by your rules. Forgive us when we break a rule, and help us to do better next time. Amen.

# 32

## Born in a Manger
## (Christmas)

**Preparation:** Have your birth certificate to show to the children.

**Key Verse:** She wrapped him in cloths and placed him in a manger, because there was no room for them in the inn (Luke 2:7b).

Does anyone know what this is? *(Allow responses.)* This is a birth certificate. A birth certificate is filled out by the doctor when a baby is born. It gives many facts about the birth. It tells the name of the baby, who his or her parents are, the name of the doctor who helped with the birth, the name of the hospital, and the date the baby was born. Let's look at this birth certificate and find all of those things. *(Look at the birth certificate with the children, pointing out the information on it.)*

When Jesus was born, he probably didn't have a birth certificate like this. But the Bible tells us many things about his birth that would be on a birth certificate. Of course the name of the baby was *Jesus.* Can anybody tell me the date of his birth? *(Allow responses.)* We don't know for sure the exact date, but we do know it happened about 4 A.D. Today we celebrate his birth on December 25. Now, can someone tell me what hospital he was born in? *(Allow responses.)* He wasn't born in a hospital, was he? Jesus was born in a stable in the town of Bethlehem. Who were Jesus' parents? *(Allow responses.)* Jesus' earthly parents were Mary and Joseph. And who was the doctor who helped with the birth? *(Allow responses.)* There was no doctor present with Mary and Joseph when Jesus was born.

Even though we don't have a certificate of Jesus' birth, the Bible tells us how it all happened. And of all the babies ever born into the world, Jesus was the most special, because Jesus is God's Son.

*Prayer:* Dear God, thank you for Jesus. And thank you for the Bible that tells us the wonderful story of his birth. Amen.

# 33

## God Is Our Strength

**Preparation:** Obtain a bowling ball or another rather heavy (but safe) object.

**Key Verse:** Look to the LORD and his strength;
seek his face always (Ps. 105:4).

I need a couple volunteers today. Does anyone want to help? *(Choose two volunteers.)* We are going to see how strong you are. I want each of you to lift this bowling ball and set it back down. The ball is pretty heavy, so it takes some strength to lift it. I'll lift it first to show you how, and then I'll let each of you try. *(Demonstrate how to lift the bowling ball. Do not lift it by the finger holes, but cradle it with both hands underneath.)* Now each of you try to lift the ball. *(Allow each volunteer to lift the ball. When they have finished, have them take their seats and resume the lesson.)*

That ball is heavy, isn't it? A person has to be pretty strong to lift it. Do you think God could lift a bowling ball? *(Allow responses.)* How many bowling balls do you think God could lift? *(Allow responses.)* God could lift as many bowling balls as he wants to, because God is stronger than anybody or anything.

It is good to be strong. You are getting stronger every day as you grow up. When you were a baby, you couldn't lift a bowling ball no matter how hard you tried. But some people think that they are strong enough to do anything. They think they don't ever need anybody to help them do anything. And they think they don't need God either.

The problem is, nobody is that strong. Everybody needs help sometime. And when we have a problem that seems too big for us, there is nobody better than God to help us. God wants to help us, and he has the strength and power to help us. The Bible says, "Look to the LORD and his strength." So when we have a problem that is too big or too hard for us, let's be sure to ask God for his help. He is strong, and he can help us.

*Prayer:* Dear Lord, we thank you for helping us with our problems. When problems are big, help us to trust in your strength. Amen.

# 34

## A Thank-you Note to God

**Preparation:** Obtain a thank-you note, and make a large thank-you note out of construction paper. On the front of the large card write the words, "I THANK YOU GOD FOR."

**Key Verse:** We give thanks to you, O God (Ps. 75:1a).

There are many ways to say thank you. One way is to write a thank-you note and give it to the person who did something nice for you. *(Show the small thank-you note.)* This is what a thank-you note looks like. I've received thank-you notes from people after I had done something for them or had given a gift. Receiving a thank-you note made me feel very happy. It is always nice to tell someone "thank you."

Today we're going to write a thank-you note to God. *(Show the large thank-you note.)* The front of this card says, "I THANK YOU GOD FOR." When we open the card there is no writing inside. Do you know why? It is because we haven't written our card yet.

God does much for us for which we should be thankful. As you tell me what you are thankful for, I will write a list on this card. What are some things you thank God for? *(As children make suggestions, write them inside the card. The list may include mothers and fathers, food, water, church, Jesus, homes, and many others.)*

There is much we are thankful for. Let me read again those we listed. *(Read them aloud.)* We could have written many more also, because God is so good to us. Let's pray together and thank God for his goodness to us.

*Prayer:* Dear God, thank you for all the good things you give to us. You are good to us, and we love you. Amen.

# 35

## Win or Lose

**Preparation:** Obtain a trophy.

**Key Verse:**  My flesh and my heart may fail,
but God is the strength of my heart
and my portion forever (Ps. 73:26).

Have any of you ever received a trophy? *(Allow responses.)* Trophies are often given after a contest. A trophy may be given for a sporting event, like a race or a baseball game. Sometimes trophies are given for other kinds of events, such as dog shows or music contests. Sometimes everyone in a contest receives a trophy. Many times, however, only the one who is judged to have done the best gets a trophy. In a race the person who won the race would get the trophy. In a dog show the prettiest, most well-behaved dog would win.

Let's pretend you were in a race. A trophy would be given for first place. How many first-place trophies would be given out? *(Allow responses.)* Only one person comes in first, and that person would receive the trophy. Everybody tried to win, but only one came in first.

We can't always come in first place. We can't always be the winner. Everybody loses sometime. Even when we do our best to win, sometimes we will lose. Losing may make us sad. It makes some people feel like they are not good for anything.

But there are a couple of thoughts to keep in mind about losing. First we should always do our best. Doing our best is more important than winning or losing. The second point to keep in mind is that God always loves us, even when we don't win. There's nothing we can do to make God stop loving us.

*Prayer:* Dear God, help us to always do our best, and thank you for always loving us the same, whether we win or lose. Amen.

# 36

# When People Don't Understand

**Preparation:** Obtain an onion.

**Key Verse:** Everyone who wants to live a godly life in Christ Jesus will be persecuted (2 Tim. 3:12).

This is an onion. Do you enjoy eating onions? Onions are good in certain foods, but most people don't eat a lot of raw onions.

Let's pretend that you really liked to eat onions. When you came home from school and were looking for something to eat, you would find an onion and take a big bite out of it. You would then go outside with your onion, and eat it while you were walking down the street. Of course some of your friends would see you eating the onion. What would they think about your eating the onion? *(Allow responses.)* Probably some of your friends would not understand why you were eating it. Some of them might even make fun of you.

Many times when people don't understand a choice you have made they will make fun of you. That doesn't mean that there is anything wrong with your choice.

There is nothing wrong with eating the onion, if you like onions. But others who don't like onions may make fun of your choice.

The Bible says that when we choose to follow Jesus, many people will not understand. They don't know about Jesus, and will not understand your choice to follow him. Since they do not understand, some people may make fun of you. But remember, just because people make fun of a choice you have made, it doesn't mean that your choice is bad. It only means that they don't understand the choice you have made. The best choice we could ever make is to be Jesus' friend. Then it really doesn't matter what people say or think about us, because we know we have made the right choice.

*Prayer:* Dear God, help us when friends don't understand the choices we make. Help us to follow you no matter what people think. Amen.

# 37

# The Most Valuable Person

**Preparation:** Obtain a few baseball cards.

**Key Verse:** Look at the birds of the air; they do not sow or reap or store away in barns, and yet your heavenly Father feeds them. Are you not much more valuable than they? (Matt. 6:26).

I have with me today a few baseball cards. Do you like baseball? *(Allow responses.)* I enjoy watching baseball games, and sometimes I play baseball, too.

Who gets their pictures on baseball cards? *(Allow responses.)* Baseball players get their pictures on baseball cards. It is fun to collect baseball cards and see how many different pictures you can get.

On the back of the card is another important item: the statistics. Statistics tell what a player has done so far in baseball. If we want to see how many hits, home runs, or stolen bases a player has, we can find out by looking at the back of the card. Let's look at a few cards. *(Read a few statistics from two or three of the cards.)*

Some players get more hits and home runs than others, don't they? The more hits and home runs a player gets, the more valuable he is to his team. At the end of the year, team members even vote to see who is the Most Valuable Player. The Most Valuable Player is the player who is more important to his team than any other player.

Do you think that God thinks of some people as more valuable than others? *(Allow responses.)* God doesn't have favorites. All people are valuable to God, because he made every person and loves every one the same. The song "Jesus Loves the Little Children" says, "Red and yellow, black and white; all are precious in his sight." And so there are no "Most Valuable People" to God, because everyone is precious to him.

*Prayer:* Dear God, thank you for loving us all the same. Help us to love one another also. Amen.

# 38

## Only One Kind of Words

**Preparation:** Obtain a dog dish.

**Key Verse:** Out of the same mouth come praise and cursing. My brothers, this should not be (James 3:10).

This is a special bowl. Do you know what it is used for? The dish belongs to my dog, and she eats out of it.

My dog really gets excited at feeding time. I go to get her food, and she starts wagging her tail as fast as she can. After I put the food in her bowl, she begins to gobble it up.

After my dog finishes eating, then I can take her dish and put my dinner in it and eat out of the same bowl! Don't you do the same thing at home? *(Allow responses.)* Well, I don't *really* eat out of the dog dish either. I was just joking with you. Dog dishes are for dogs' use. The proper use for dog dishes is only for dogs.

There are other items we use every day that are to be used only in one way. Does your mother make soup in the trash can? *(Allow responses.)* Of course not. A trash can is for trash and not anything else. Do you brush your teeth with a comb? *(Allow responses.)* No, a comb is only for combing hair. Are we supposed to say bad words with our mouths? *(Allow responses.)* The Bible says that some people use their mouths to say both good and bad words, but that's not what God wants. God wants us to use our mouths to say only good things. Just as a dog dish is to be used for only one kind of food—dog food—so our mouths are to be used for only one kind of words—good words.

*Prayer:* Lord, help us to say only good words with our mouths—words of kindness and love. Amen.

# 39

## Persistence

**Preparation:** Obtain a putter, a golf ball, and a practice putting cup. Ask a volunteer to help with this lesson. Set the cup on the floor, and the ball about fifteen feet away.

**Key Verse:** Let us not become weary in doing good, for at the proper time we will reap a harvest if we do not give up (Gal. 6:9).

I've asked *[name of volunteer]* to help us today. He likes to golf, and so I've asked him to show us how to putt the golf ball. We will count to see how many times it takes him to get the ball into the practice cup. *(Direct the volunteer to putt the ball in the cup. Have him continue hitting until he makes it into the cup. Count with the children how many putts it takes.)*

Well he made it. How many tries did it take before he put the ball in the cup? *(Allow responses.)* He didn't make it on his first try, did he? What if he had quit after his first try? *(Allow responses.)* If he had quit too soon, he wouldn't have made it into the cup.

Sometimes we quit too soon doing other things also. You may be reading a book, get tired, and quit before you finished the story. You will never know how the story turns out unless you continue reading. You may be helping your father wash the car, get tired, and quit before the car is completely washed.

The Bible tells us not to quit too soon. It says, "Do not become weary in doing good." That means we should finish the job we started and not give up. We shouldn't quit when the job gets hard or when we get bored. We should "stick with it" until the job is finished.

*Prayer:* Dear God, help us to finish the jobs we begin. Help us to do our best even when the job is hard. Amen.

# 40

## Mothers Are Special (Mother's Day)

**Preparation:** Obtain a rose.

**Key Verse:** Honor your father and mother (Eph. 6:2a).

I have a rose with me today. The rose is the favorite of all the flowers in the world. How many roses do you think there are in the world? *(Allow responses.)* Nobody knows exactly how many roses there are in the world, but we do know more than 50 million American families grow at least one rosebush at home. That's a lot of rosebushes, isn't it?

It would be hard to imagine a world without flowers, wouldn't it? Flowers are pretty, they smell nice, and they bring happiness when they are given to someone. All the different colors of flowers in the world make the world a more beautiful place. God did a good thing when he made flowers.

Today is Mother's Day. Mothers are a little like flowers. They are pretty, smell nice, and bring happiness, much like a flower does. But they are different in one big way. There are millions of flowers in the world. If you took a walk around the block in your neighborhood, you might be able to count one hundred or more flowers. There are many flowers all around you, but you only have one mother who loves and takes care of you. Mothers are special, because God gives us only one.

Since our mothers are special to us, we should treat them special. The Bible says, "Honor your father and mother." Mothers are to be loved, respected, and obeyed.

Yes, God did a good thing when he made flowers. But God did something extra-special when he made mothers. Let's thank God for our mothers.

*Prayer:* Dear God, thank you for our mothers. Help us to honor them this day and every day. Amen.

# 41

# We Are Made by God

**Preparation:** Obtain some modeling clay.

**Key Verse:** The LORD God formed man from the dust of the ground and breathed into his nostrils the breath of life, and man became a living being (Gen. 2:7).

Today I need a volunteer. *(Pick a boy or girl.)* I have some clay with me today. I want you to take the clay and make whatever you want to with it. Of course you'll have to make it rather quickly—but go ahead and make something out of the clay.

*(As the volunteer is making something, discuss clay with the other children. Ask such questions as "Do you like playing with clay?" "Do you know where clay comes from?" "What do you like to make from clay?")*

Okay, let's see what he [or she] has made. Can you tell about what you have made? *(Allow the volunteer to respond.)* That's very nice. Did you enjoy working with the clay? *(Allow responses.)*

The Bible tells us that God made the whole world. I think when he made the world, he had as much fun making it as we have playing with clay.

But God did something with what he made that we can't do. God gave life to the things he made. All the trees, plants, fish, animals, and people were given life by God. We can't do that when we make objects, because only God can give life.

Let's thank God for his wonderful world, and for giving us life so that we can enjoy it.

*Prayer:* Dear God, thank you for making the world. Thank you for giving us life and letting us enjoy your world. Amen.

# 42

## Words of Kindness

**Preparation:** Obtain a dictionary.

**Key Verse:**     May the words of my mouth and the
            meditation of my heart
            be pleasing in your sight,
            O LORD, my Rock and my Redeemer
            (Ps. 19:14).

A dictionary is very useful. A dictionary is a book that has thousands of words in it. It shows us how to spell each word correctly and also tells us what each word means.

Let me show you what I mean. I'll tell you a word in the dictionary, and you tell me what the word means. The word is *factotum*. Does anyone know what *factotum* means? *(Allow responses.)* Factotum is a person who knows how to do all kinds of work. Another word for factotum is a handyman. The dictionary also tells us that factotum is spelled f-a-c-t-o-t-u-m.

There are so many words in the dictionary, it would be difficult to learn them all. Words are wonderful because if it were not for words, we could not talk to each other.

But the Bible reminds us also that words can be used to hurt people. If we call people mean names or say things that hurt people's feelings, we haven't used words in ways that please God. God wants us to be kind to one another, and for our words to be pleasing to God, they must be words of kindness.

Psalm 19:14 says, "May the words of my mouth and the meditation of my heart be pleasing in your sight, O Lord." Whatever we say and whatever we think needs to please God. So let's be careful what we say to one another, being sure that all our words are kind.

*Prayer:* Lord, help us to say words that help people, not hurt people. Help us to be kind to others. Amen.

# 43

## Jesus' Love Is Indescribable

**Preparation:** Gift wrap a shoe box. Wrap it so that the lid can be removed. Inside the box place three small items that would be appropriate gifts for children (a toy car, small stuffed animal, a bag of marbles, and so forth).

**Key Verse:** Thanks be to God for his indescribable gift! (2 Cor. 9:15).

This is a box decorated for giving a gift to someone. Inside the box are three items that someone might give to someone else as a gift. We're going to take one thing out of the box at a time, and describe it. Do you know what *describe* means? *(Allow responses.)* When we describe something, we tell about it. We might tell what it looks like, what it feels like, or how big it is.

Let's take out one of the items and describe it. This is a little stuffed animal. Who can describe it for me? *(Allow responses. You may have to ask leading questions, such as, "What color is it?" "What does it feel like?")* If someone gave us this stuffed animal as a gift, we could easily describe it, couldn't we?

Let's take out something else from the box. This is a bag of marbles. Who can describe these marbles to me? *(Allow responses. Again, ask leading questions as necessary, such as, "What shape are the marbles?" "What color are the marbles?")* If we received these marbles as a gift, we would have no problem describing them, would we?

Let's take one more item from the box and describe it. This is a toy car. Who can describe the car for me? *(Allow responses. Once again, ask leading questions if necessary, such as, "How many wheels does it have?" "How big is it?")* If someone gave us this car as a gift, we could describe it to someone else, couldn't we?

Most items (or people) are easy to describe. But the Bible tells of one gift that is impossible to describe. The Bible says, "Thanks be to God for his indescribable gift!" What gift do you think the Bible is talking about? *(Allow responses.)* The Bible is talking about Jesus. God sent Jesus into the world because he loved the world. But Jesus is so special, there are no words special enough to describe all about him. And so when we tell about Jesus, we do our best to describe how special he is to us, but nothing we can say can tell how great and wonderful he is. Jesus is special beyond any words we can say.

*Prayer:* Dear God, thank you for the gift of Jesus. Jesus is very special, and we love him very much. Thank you for sending him into our world. Amen.

# 44

## Two Special Words

**Preparation:** Have enough bite-sized candies for each child to have one.

**Key Verse:** He threw himself at Jesus' feet and thanked him (Luke 17:16a).

Today I have something to give to each of you. *(Give a piece of candy to each child.)* What do you say when someone gives you something? *(Allow responses.)* That's right, we say, "Thank you." When someone gives you something or does something nice for you, it is good to say, "Thank you."

The Bible tells a story which teaches us about saying *thank you.* One day Jesus was walking along the road. As he was walking, ten men who were very sick met him. They had a terrible disease called *leprosy.* They asked if Jesus would make them well, because they had heard that Jesus could heal people.

Jesus was happy to help these people. He made them well, and all ten of the men went on their way, happy and excited that they were well again. But one of the men remembered that he had not said *thank you* to

Jesus. He went back to find Jesus, and when he found him what do you think he did? *(Allow responses.)* He told Jesus "thank you" for making him well again.

Jesus said, "Where are the other nine?" He had healed ten men, but only one returned to say, "Thank you." He was happy that this man returned to say thanks, but sad that the others did not.

Jesus teaches us that we should say *thank you* to people who are nice to us. So let's not forget those two special words that make people happy: *thank you*.

*Prayer:* Dear God, thank you for your love and for all you do for us. Help us to remember to say *thank you* to others every day. Amen.

# 45

## God Is Our Protection

**Preparation:** Obtain a pair of leather gloves and a tumbleweed (or other weed with prickers).

**Key Verse:** You will protect me from trouble (Ps. 32:7b).

Look what blew into my backyard last week: a tumbleweed! I was not very happy to have it in my yard. A tumbleweed doesn't look that nice next to the pretty rosebushes and other green plants.

Since I did not want the tumbleweed in my yard, I decided I would throw it in the trash. But do you know what happened when I went to pick it up? It stuck me! Tumbleweeds have sharp thorns (or prickers), and one stuck in my finger.

I knew then that I could not pick up the tumbleweed with my bare hands. I needed something to protect my hands so I wouldn't get pricked again. I found my leather gloves in the garage. I put them on and tried again to pick up the tumbleweed. Guess what happened this time? I was able to pick up the tumbleweed without getting any prickers because the gloves were protecting my hands.

Sometimes things other than thorns try to hurt us. The devil may try to hurt us with evil. Just as our hands need extra help to be protected from a tumbleweed, so we need extra help to be protected from the devil and his evil.

The Bible says that God will protect us from trouble. We don't need to worry about the devil as long as we believe in God. He will keep us from getting hurt.

*Prayer:* Dear God, thank you for protecting us and keeping us safe. Amen.

# 46

## The Bible Is Our Guide

**Preparation:** Obtain a *TV Guide* magazine and a Bible.

**Key Verse:**     Your word is a lamp to my feet
and a light for my path (Ps. 119:105).

Today I have with me a *TV Guide*. Do you all know what a *TV Guide* is used for? It helps us make decisions about what to watch on television. Let's see how it works. We will turn to Saturday morning at 9:00 and read all the television shows that are listed for that time. We then can choose which show we would like to watch. *(Turn in the* TV Guide *to Saturday 9:00 A.M. and read the list of shows.)* Which of those shows listed would you like to watch the most? *(Allow responses.)* TV Guide is helpful for making decisions about watching television.

I have another kind of guide with me also. *(Hold up the Bible.)* This is a Bible. The Bible helps us make decisions about choices in life. We can call it our life guide.

Let's compare the *TV Guide* with the Bible, our life guide. *TV Guide* is written by people about television. The Bible is written by people directed by God. It tells about God's love for us. *TV Guide* is good for only one week. After that the shows on television change and a new *TV Guide* must be written. The Bible is good forever and ever. No matter what kind of changes happen in the world, the Bible is still up to date.

Which do you think is the more valuable book, the Bible or the *TV Guide. (Allow responses.)* Yes, the Bible is far more valuable. Let's thank God for the Bible, our life guide.

*Prayer:* Dear God, thank you for the Bible. Help us to use it to guide our lives. Amen.

# 47

# God Understands Everything

**Preparation:** Obtain a glass, a 3″ x 5″ index card, and a 9″ x 13″ cake pan. Fill the glass nearly full with water. Place the index card on the top of the glass. Carefully holding the card to the rim of the glass, turn the glass completely upside down. Slowly remove your hand from the card. The water should remain in the glass. Practice this before trying it with the children. Do the demonstration over a cake pan, so that if it fails, the water will fall into the pan instead of on the floor!

**Key Verse:** Great is our Lord and mighty in power; his understanding has no limit (Ps. 147:5a).

When I was a little boy, there were a lot of things I didn't understand. I couldn't wait until I grew up so that I would understand everything. I thought all grown-ups understood everything.

When I grew up, though, I found there was still a lot I didn't understand. Let me show you something. I'm going to take this glass filled with ordinary water, put a card on top of the glass, turn the glass over, and let go of the card. What do you think will happen when I let go of the card? *(Allow responses.)* Well, let's see what happens. *(Do the trick described above.)*

The water remained in the glass, didn't it? I don't understand why the water stayed in the glass but it did. This is just one thing I don't understand. There is much more in life I can't figure out. But it is okay that we don't understand everything in life. Do you know why? It is because God understands everything. The Bible says his understanding has no limit. And so when I don't understand something, I can still trust in God knowing that *he* understands everything.

*Prayer:* Dear God, help us to trust in you even when something happens that we don't understand. Amen.

# 48

## Our Gift to Jesus (Advent)

**Preparation:** Gift wrap a shoe box in Christmas wrapping paper. Wrap the lid of the box separately, so that it can be taken off. Write the following words or phrases on 3" x 5" index cards with a felt marker (one word or phrase per card): LOVE; OFFERING; TIME IN PRAYER; TIME HELPING OTHERS; TIME IN CHURCH AND SUNDAY SCHOOL; FIGHTING WITH BROTHERS OR SISTERS; COVETING; DISOBEDIENCE TO PARENTS; DISHONESTY.

**Key Verse:** On coming to the house, they saw the child with his mother Mary, and they bowed down and worshiped him. Then they opened their treasures and presented him with gifts of gold and of incense and of myrrh (Matt. 2:11).

Christmas is coming. At Christmastime many people will be giving and receiving presents. We give presents to show that we love other people. When the wise men came to see the baby Jesus they gave him gifts to show that they loved him, and so we give gifts at Christmas to show our love also.

Christmas is Jesus' birthday. Don't you think we should give Jesus a present on his birthday? We love Jesus, and can show Jesus our love by what we give to him.

Here is a box all decorated for Christmas. There is nothing inside the box yet. You will help me decide what we should put in the box to give to Jesus.

Here is a card that says TIME IN PRAYER. Can we give Jesus time in prayer? (Allow responses.) Jesus would like us to spend time in prayer, for that is how we talk to him. Let's put it in the box.

This card says DISHONESTY. Do you think dishonesty makes Jesus happy? (Allow responses.) Let's not give Jesus dishonesty.

This card says OFFERING. Do you think it is good to give an offering in Sunday school or church? (Allow responses.) Offerings help us send missionaries to tell others about Jesus. I think Jesus likes that. Let's put OFFERING in the box.

TIME HELPING OTHERS is what this card says. Do you think helping others would make Jesus happy? (Allow responses.) It would make him happy, so we'll put it in our gift box for him.

Here is a card that says FIGHTING WITH BROTHERS OR SISTERS. That wouldn't make Jesus very happy, would it? We won't give that to Jesus.

TIME IN CHURCH AND SUNDAY SCHOOL is written on this card. Would Jesus like us to be in church and Sunday school? (Allow responses.) We learn about Jesus and worship him in church and Sunday school. I'm sure he likes that. We'll put it in the box.

This card says COVETING. Coveting happens when we want something another person has, and we wish we had it instead of him. Would coveting make Jesus happy? *(Allow responses.)* No, Jesus doesn't like us to covet, so we will leave it out of the box.

Here is a card that says DISOBEDIENCE TO PARENTS. Does Jesus like it when we don't obey our mothers and fathers? *(Allow responses.)* The Bible says children are to obey their parents. Disobedience would not please Jesus, so we won't put it in the gift box.

Can anyone read the last card? *(Allow responses.)* The last card says LOVE. Do you think Jesus would like to receive our love? *(Allow responses.)* Our love would make Jesus very happy. Let's include it in our gift to Jesus.

Let's read all the cards we put in the box: TIME IN CHURCH AND SUNDAY SCHOOL; TIME HELPING OTHERS; TIME IN PRAYER; OFFERING; and LOVE. Jesus will be happy as we do all these. I'm sure that Jesus will like his present from us.

*Prayer:* Dear Jesus, we wish you a happy birthday at Christmastime. Accept the gifts we give you today. Thank you for always loving us. Amen.

# 49

## The Freedoms We Enjoy (Independence Day)

**Preparation:** Obtain a newspaper, a microphone, and a Bible.

**Key Verse:** I will walk about in freedom,
for I have sought out your precepts
(Ps. 119:45).

Today we celebrate our country's Independence Day. The USA is a wonderful country in which to live, because people who live in America enjoy many freedoms that some people in other countries cannot enjoy.

A very important piece of paper in the United States is known as the "Bill of Rights." The Bill of Rights tells about the many freedoms that Americans have.

I have brought with me three items that the Bill of Rights tells about. The first is a *newspaper*. The Bill of Rights says that we are allowed to write and read newspapers. Do you know that there are some countries where writing or reading newspapers is against the law? It would be strange to live in a place where we would be afraid to read a newspaper.

The second item I have is a *microphone*. The microphone stands for what the Bill of Rights calls "freedom of speech." That means that we are allowed to say what we think without having to be afraid. Do you know that in some countries people are put in jail for saying what they think? That wouldn't be good at all.

The last item I have is a *Bible*. In our country we can worship God without being afraid or having to do it in secret. People in some countries cannot worship God without being afraid that they will get caught and get into trouble. It is wonderful that we can worship God without worry or fear.

We do live in a great country, don't we? We should enjoy living in the United States of America, and thank God for giving us a country in which we can read newspapers, say what we think, and especially, where we can worship God.

*Prayer:* Thank you, God, for our country, and for the many freedoms we enjoy. Amen.

# 50

## Doing Good for Others (Maundy Thursday)

**Preparation:** Obtain a towel and a bucket.

**Key Verse:**  I have set you an example that you should do as I have done for you (John 13:15).

I'm going to tell you a true story about the objects I have today. This is a towel and a bucket. One day Jesus used a towel and a bucket in a way that surprised his friends.

Jesus was in a room with his friends having dinner. As everyone was beginning to eat, Jesus got up, took a towel and bucket of water, and began washing the feet of his friends.

In Bible days, people wore sandals and traveled by walking. The roads were made of dirt, and so people's feet would become dirty when they walked from one place to another. Jesus was doing a very helpful thing for his friends as he washed the dirt from their feet.

But Jesus' friends were embarrassed. Finally Peter said, "You're not going to wash my feet." Jesus said, "If you are my friends, you will let me wash your feet." Peter was Jesus' friend, and so he changed his mind and let Jesus wash his feet.

When Jesus had finished washing the feet of all his friends he asked, "Do you know why I washed your feet?" Then he told his friends, "It is because I love you and want to do things for you. You, also, should love others and do nice things for them."

Jesus' friends remembered what he said. We are Jesus' friends too. Since we are his friends, we should show our love for others by helping them and being nice to them.

*Prayer:* Dear God, thank you for being so good to us. Help us to show our love to others by being kind to them. Amen.